TO: Tisha

**LOVE
FROM:** Gina ☺

Dedicated to Alicia

Text copyright © 1997 Julie Mitchell Marra
Photography copyright © 1997 NBM Bahner Studios, AG
All rights reserved.
Licensed by Alaska Momma,™ Inc.

No part of this book may be reproduced in any form or by any means,
electronic or mechanical, including photocopying, recording, or by any information
storage or retrieval system without the written permission of the publisher.

Design by Anderson Thomas Design

Published by C.R. Gibson®
C.R. Gibson® is a registered trademark of Thomas Nelson, Inc.
Nashville, Tennessee 37214

Printed in Mexico.

ISBN 0-7667-6650-0
GB649R

To My Sister

photographs by
KIM ANDERSON

poetry by
JULIE MITCHELL MARRA

Without you,

GROWING

would not have been the same.

OVER THE YEARS

Over the years

we have shared so much

and built a relationship

that is precious and lasting.

WE HAVE SHARED

ice cream at the beach, popcorn at the movies,

and hot dogs on the sidewalk.

We have shared amusement park rides,

splashing in puddles in the rain, sledding, skating –

and making angels in the snow.

With you I can laugh, I can cry,

I can say what's on my mind

or just be silent.

WITH YOU
it's easy to be me.

I remember disagreements . . .

saying things we didn't really mean.

I also remember that

only hours later

we were *l a u g h i n g*

so hard we cried.

SOMETIMES WHEN
life seems difficult...

I remember our childhood days

full of laughter and love.

Then I am able to lift my spirits

and *lighten* my outlook.

The memories we share

remind me of how lucky I am

to have a *sister* like you.

People we meet see

a little of you in me

and a little of me in you.

I   l o o k   a t   y o u

and my eyes look back.

I   s p e a k

and I hear your voice.

WE ARE MORE
than merely acquaintances...

it's as if we are cut from the same fabric.

We have a common thread that won't be broken –

by people or years or distance.

WE ARE NEVER
at a loss for words.

We can talk for hours

about nothing at all or communicate

the deepest hurt with a *s i n g l e* word.

With you, speech is effortless and laughter is contagious.

You bring love and light, kindness and caring,

cheer and *s u p p o r t* into my life.

WE DO NOT ALWAYS SEE

eye to eye...

Sometimes we take different roads.

Our relationship is not always perfect,

but when we have a problem it's surmountable.

Sometimes we are the mirror image

of each other and other times

we couldn't be more opposite.

But because of you, I know myself better.

I know that if I pick up
the phone, *you'll be there.*

If I need help, you'll
give it to me *twofold.*

If I start to go down the wrong path,
you'll try to *lead me* the right way.

There's no end to what you do for me
and I want you to know I'll *do the same for you.*

Thank you for listening without judging,

and for giving advice without pushing.

Thank you for helping

me gain confidence in myself

to stand alone –

and for letting me know you'll

always be there.

The greatest part about being sisters

SHARING

is *s h a r i n g* ourselves.

Having our own interests,

COMMUNICATING

but always *c o m m u n i c a t i n g.*

Striving to meet our own goals,

SIGHT

but never losing *s i g h t* of one another.

Living our own lives,

CONNECTED

but always remaining *c o n n e c t e d.*

You and I have so many memories . . .

you share my history.

You remember where I've been,

respect who I've become,

and encourage me where I'm going.

I know that our relationship will

grow stronger year after year.

And I hope that all of the blessings

you bring to my life –

I can return to you.

May you always be fulfilled.

May you feel content with

your accomplishments

and, no matter what,

know that you are

truly and deeply loved.

YOU ARE MY SISTER
and my best friend!